VIOLENCE
AGAINST
WOMEN

BY SHERRI MABRY GORDON

ReferencePoint
Press®

San Diego, CA

© 2019 ReferencePoint Press, Inc.
Printed in the United States

For more information, contact:
ReferencePoint Press, Inc.
PO Box 27779
San Diego, CA 92198
www.ReferencePointPress.com

LIBRARY OF CONGRESS CATALOGING-IN-PUBLICATION DATA

Name: Gordon, Sherri Mabry, author.
Title: Violence Against Women/by Sherri Mabry Gordon.
Description: San Diego, CA: ReferencePoint Press, Inc., [2019] | Series: Women and Society
| Audience: Grade 9 to 12 | Includes bibliographical references and index.
ISBN: 978-1-68282-545-7 (hardback)
ISBN: 978-1-68282-546-4 (ebook)
The complete Library of Congress record is available at www.loc.gov.

CONTENTS

IMPORTANT EVENTS IN
WOMEN'S HISTORY

1915
Women from the United States and Europe gather in the Netherlands for the first International Congress of Women.

1977
The White Buffalo Calf Women Society is founded at the Rosebud Sioux Reservation in the United States. It's the first nonprofit for American Indian women who are victims of violence.

1871
Alabama is the first state to rescind men's legal right to beat their wives.

1967
One of the United States' first women's shelters for domestic violence victims opens in Maine.

1890   **1910**   **1930**   **1950**   **1970**

1946
The United Nations (UN) Commission on the Status of Women is established. It mandates that standards be set for women's rights.

1911
In March, the first-ever International Women's Day is celebrated.

1978
Both the National Coalition Against Sexual Assault and the National Coalition Against Domestic Violence are formed in the United States.

1972
The first rape crisis line in the United States is opened in Washington, DC.

2009
Barack Obama is the first US president to declare April as Sexual Assault Awareness Month.

2017
In October, the international #MeToo movement against sexual harassment and sexual assault is launched, creating a platform for survivors to speak out.

1985
The US surgeon general identifies domestic violence as a public health issue.

1980   **1990**   **2000**   **2010**   **2020**

1984
The US Congress passes the Family Violence Prevention Services Act. It's the first time that federal funds are designated specifically for domestic violence programs.

1996
The VAWA funds the National Domestic Violence Hotline (1-800-799-SAFE) and takes its first call on February 21. The hotline answers nearly 4,900 calls in its first month.

2012
The UN passes a historic resolution outlawing female genital mutilation.

2008
A UN resolution recognizes that sexual violence can be categorized as a war crime and calls for protection from violence in refugee camps.

1990
US senator Joe Biden introduces the first Violence Against Women Act (VAWA) in the United States.

A SPOTLIGHT ON VIOLENCE AGAINST WOMEN

||||

There is a lot of misinformation and stereotyping about violence against women. Some people mistakenly envision the victims only as poor, uneducated women or perhaps only women in developing countries. People may think "not in my neighborhood" or "not in my family," believing that the women they know could never be faced with violence. But the truth is that abuse can happen to any woman, at any age, of any race, and within any income bracket. Take for instance four New York women, including a successful attorney, a published author, and a political activist. At a glance, no one would have expected that they were victims of violence. But that is exactly what happened to them. All four accused New York's attorney general, Eric Schneiderman, of sexual abuse in May 2018. Schneiderman resigned from that job amid the allegations.

Empowered by the #MeToo movement, in which women around the world began publicly sharing their stories of abuse and harassment in late 2017, Schneiderman's alleged victims decided it was time to share their stories as well. As a result, they publicly accused Schneiderman of physical violence including strangulation and brutal beatings, threats of violence, controlling behaviors, and more. One of the women's stories was recounted in the *New Yorker*. The magazine wrote that in the early stages of her relationship with him, "Schneiderman made an advance toward her [but] when she rebuffed him, he slapped her across the face with such force that it left a mark that lingered the next day. She recalls screaming in surprise and pain, and beginning to cry, and says that she felt frightened."[1]

"Schneiderman made an advance toward her [but] when she rebuffed him, he slapped her across the face with such force that it left a mark that lingered the next day. She recalls screaming in surprise and pain, and beginning to cry, and says that she felt frightened."[1]
– *the* New Yorker

Aside from the brutality he is accused of, what makes the Schneiderman case even more shocking is that he had long been considered a champion of women's rights. He even rewrote legislation that established stiffer penalties for strangulation, predicting that it would save lives. This work made the reports that he was engaging in strangulation behind closed doors seem even more surprising. Jennifer Friedman, a legal expert on domestic violence, said that Schneiderman's public and private behaviors don't make sense. Anyone who is educated on domestic violence knows that strangulation is "a known lethality indicator," Friedman told the *New Yorker*. "I cannot fathom that someone who *drafted* the legislation on strangulation is unfamiliar with such concepts."[2]

One of Schneiderman's alleged victims also had trouble making sense of his actions and described him as "a Dr. Jekyll and Mr. Hyde."[3] The *New Yorker* explained that "seeing him lauded as a supporter of women has made her 'feel sick.'"[4] She added, "This is a man who staked his entire

Eric Schneiderman spoke as New York's attorney general at the Women's March in New York City in January 2018, months before he resigned from his position after allegations of sexual abuse. Four women accused Schneiderman in May 2018 of repeated sexual abuse.

career, his personal narrative, on being a champion for women publicly. But he abuses them privately. He needs to be called out."[5]

It is not uncommon for abusive men to have two different sides to their personalities—a side they reserve for the public eye and a side they keep hidden. Although many people assume that stress, anger, and even alcohol cause violence, the truth is that violence against women is a choice, and perpetrators use violence to control victims. It is about "an abusive partner *using* their control, not *losing* their control," according to SAFE, a domestic violence prevention organization in Austin, Texas. "Their actions are almost always deliberate."[6]

What's more, the men who are perpetrating this violence are almost always in a position of power. Whether it is in the workplace, in the community, or in the home, they have more power than women, and they use it to their advantage, actress Rose McGowan said. McGowan's story about being raped by famous Hollywood producer Harvey Weinstein was a catalyst behind the #MeToo movement.

"Power is a many-headed beast—it's the hydra," McGowan said. "You put one down and another one pops up."[7] In reality, she added, powerful men like Weinstein and Schneiderman are just a few of the countless men who take advantage of the power they have. "We've all worked with the rot. We've all had these people," she said. "You could work at a parking garage or at a grocery store and have the same power structure, just in a different form. It could be a tiny town and this person's power in the town is omnipotent. It's really [equivalent] to power abuse and bullying."[8]

> "You could work at a parking garage or at a grocery store and have the same power structure, just in a different form. It could be a tiny town and this person's power in the town is omnipotent. It's really [equivalent] to power abuse and bullying."[8]
> – Rose McGowan, actress and activist

What's worse is that the actions of these men are often deliberate, author Kate Manne wrote in the *New York Times*. "A dark but important truth about [violence against women is that] some abusers are . . . well aware of what they are doing, at least at a certain level. And that is why they keep doing it," she wrote. "They want to maintain dominance and exercise control over their female partners."[9]

Actress and activist Rose McGowan has spoken out about sexual harassment and sexual assault against women. She and actress Ashley Judd publicly accused Hollywood producer Harvey Weinstein of a pattern of sexual harassment, eventually leading to Weinstein's arrest in 2018.

And while there have been significant efforts toward building awareness of the frequency and severity of violence against women with movements like #MeToo, there is still much work to be done. Women are still being treated violently all around the world. In fact, roughly one-third of women in developed countries report having experienced at least one abusive relationship. And, about one in three women worldwide has experienced either physical or sexual violence in her lifetime.

McGowan has said she is worried that people might expect too much from the #MeToo movement. While the movement is getting people to talk and think about sexual harassment and violence, it will take time for things to change. She encourages people to keep sharing their stories but to be patient and not expect immediate results. For instance, she compared the campaign to the civil rights movement, which has spanned many years. While the civil rights movement started in the nineteenth century and peaked in the 1950s and 1960s, its work is ongoing. Progress on that front is continuing in today's Black Lives Matter movement. With the #MeToo movement, "This is the first time since the dawn of the caveman era that women are actually being believed," McGowan said, "and it might take hundreds of us before we're believed."[10]

CHAPTER ONE

WHAT IS THE HISTORY BEHIND VIOLENCE AGAINST WOMEN?

In 1777, a wealthy twenty-seven-year-old widow in England named Mary Eleanor Bowes was tricked into marrying an Irish man, Andrew Robinson Stoney. To win Bowes's hand in marriage, Stoney faked a duel in which he defended her honor but appeared to be seriously wounded in the process. As the story goes, Bowes was so moved by the fact that Stoney defended her that she rushed to his bedside, where he appeared to be on the verge of death.

As she sat with him, Bowes became caught up in the emotion of Stoney's actions and agreed to marry him even though he seemed so close to dying. After all, "What harm could possibly ensue from marrying a poor dying soldier who would shortly make her a widow again?" wrote Wendy Moore, author of *Wedlock: The True Story of the Disastrous Marriage and Remarkable Divorce of Mary Eleanor Bowes, Countess of Strathmore.*[11] But Stoney's injuries were all a lie. Once the wedding vows were spoken, Stoney made a miraculous recovery.

In the 1700s and 1800s, women were considered the property of their husbands. There was little that a woman could do to stop her husband from abusing her.

As a result, "Mary was about to discover the true extent of the trap into which she had been lured," Moore wrote.[12] Stoney, who changed his name to Bowes, beat Bowes with sticks, whips, and candlesticks. He also tore out her hair, burned her face, and even threatened her with knives. The beatings were frequent and merciless, and yet, Moore explained, "Mary knew that there was little she could do in her defense" because "during the eighteenth century wife-beating was not only common and widely tolerated but even supported by the law."[13]

In fact, in Georgian England, a husband was legally entitled to strike his wife to correct her behavior. One judge, Francis Buller, even went so far as to say that "a husband could beat his wife with a stick so long as it was no thicker than his thumb."[14] This statement earned him the nickname Judge Thumb. Even when violence against women exceeded what was permitted by judges like Buller, there was not much that wives could legally do to address this mistreatment. This is why what Bowes did next was so unheard of at the time. After eight long years of torture, Bowes finally escaped. Terrified, she ran from her home and her husband, and she took legal steps to pursue a divorce, get custody of her children, and reclaim her belongings from before the marriage. But her husband would not give in easily. He tracked down Bowes and kidnapped her from a London street. After eight days in captivity, she was finally rescued.

Eventually, Bowes went on to win her divorce through two appeals in court. She also regained custody of her children and reclaimed her property. When her divorce case was finally resolved in the church courts in 1786, it was among only a handful of successful cases initiated by women. Meanwhile, Bowes's husband spent the rest of his life in jail for what a local newspaper described as "barbarity that shocks humanity and outrages civilization."[15]

In 1800, just before Bowes died, she asked for "the blindfolded figure of Justice to stand guard at her tomb."[16] And although Bowes's successful divorce was remarkable for the time, it did little to help other women in similar situations. In fact, it would be nearly another century before women even received minimal legal protection against violent husbands.

ALLOWING VIOLENCE AGAINST WOMEN

Violence against women was condoned throughout history. For instance, more than 2,000 years ago, Roman law gave a man life and death authority over his wife. The eighteenth-century rule that gave men permission to discipline their wives with a stick or whip smaller than their

COULD SUPPRESSING OXYTOCIN REDUCE THE RISK OF VIOLENCE?

Research suggests that oxytocin, a chemical naturally found in the body, may increase the likelihood that men with underlying aggressive tendencies will act out and hurt their romantic partners. In fact, the hormone, often called the "love hormone" or the "cuddle hormone," signals to the brain that people should keep their partners close.

In most relationships, the hormone has a positive impact on the couple. But when one partner is predisposed to violence, this may cause him to resort to physical and emotional abuse because intimidating his wife or girlfriend is the only way he knows how to keep her from leaving. C. Nathan DeWall, a University of Kentucky psychologist who led a study on this topic, said, "Oxytocin may have diversified effects, increasing the likelihood that people who are inclined toward physical aggression will inflict harm on their romantic partners."

Overall, the study, published in the journal *Social Psychological and Personality Science,* causes researchers to wonder if the risk of violence against women could be reduced if scientists found a way to suppress oxytocin in people.

Quoted in Tom Jacobs, *"The Biological Roots of Domestic Violence,"* Pacific Standard, *February 21, 2014. www.psmag.com.*

thumbs remained law in England and in America until the late nineteenth century. Even in the twentieth century, most people considered wife beating a custom until the late 1960s and early 1970s when the feminist movement began.

"The police ignored what went on behind closed doors and women hid their bruises beneath layers of make-up," says Ruth Rosen, a fellow at the Institute for the Study of Social Change and author of *The World Split Open: How the Modern Women's Movement Changed America.* "Like rape or abortion, wife beating was viewed as a private and shameful act which few women discussed. Many battered

"The police ignored what went on behind closed doors and women hid their bruises beneath layers of make-up. Like rape or abortion, wife beating was viewed as a private and shameful act which few women discussed."[17]
– *Ruth Rosen, author of* The World Split Open: How the Modern Women's Movement Changed America

victims, moreover, felt they 'deserved' to be beaten—because they acted too uppity, didn't get dinner on the table on time, or couldn't silence their children's shouts and screams."[17]

Even doctors and other medical professionals had skewed views on violence. For instance, a 1964 article in *Time* magazine highlighted a study that concluded that "'wife beating' was therapeutic."[18] The doctors had said, "periods of violent behavior by the husband . . . served to release him momentarily from his anxiety about his ineffectiveness as a man while giving his wife apparent masochistic gratification and helping probably to deal with the guilt arising from the intense hostility expressed in her controlling, castrating behavior."[19]

The legal system also served as a roadblock for many women. For instance, up until 1976, marital rape was legal in every state in the country. Even today, a relatively small number of reported rapes end in convictions. Overall, instances of rape and sexual assault are underreported. Many victims of violence, including victims of sexual assault and rape, find the US criminal justice system difficult to navigate. Other sexual assault victims simply find it traumatizing to tell and retell their stories to police officers and in court testimony, and this can discourage them from reporting the crime.

DEFINING VIOLENCE AGAINST WOMEN

Violence is often a tactic used by one person to maintain dominance over another person. Most of the time, this violence is perpetrated by men. Consequently, though the phrase *violence against women* refers to all violent acts directed toward women, these violent acts are primarily, and sometimes exclusively, committed by men. The United Nations (UN), an international peacekeeping organization, defines *violence against women* as "any act of gender-based violence that results in, or is likely to result in, physical, sexual or mental harm or suffering to women, including threats

Rape and sexual assault are often not reported to the police. Many say this is because victims of these crimes find the criminal justice system to be traumatizing or difficult to navigate.

of such acts, coercion or arbitrary deprivation of liberty, whether occurring in public or in private life."[20] The UN Declaration on the Elimination of Violence against Women says:

> *Violence against women is a manifestation of historically unequal power relations between men and women, which have led to domination over and discrimination against women by men and to*

the prevention of the full advancement of women, and that violence against women is one of the crucial social mechanisms by which women are forced into a subordinate position compared with men.[21]

Overall, "the legacy of violence against women is tied to the history of women being viewed as property and assigned a gender role that is subservient to men," says Jane Doe Inc., the Massachusetts Coalition Against Sexual Assault and Domestic Violence.[22]

> "The legacy of violence against women is tied to the history of women being viewed as property and assigned a gender role that is subservient to men."[22]
> *– Jane Doe Inc., the Massachusetts Coalition Against Sexual Assault and Domestic Violence*

Consequently, this violence takes many forms, including domestic violence, dating violence, rape, sexual assault, sexual harassment, and human trafficking. Outside of the United States, primarily in some developing countries, women may experience genital mutilation or forced marriage. The most common type of violence that women experience is domestic violence, sometimes called intimate-partner violence.

Violence violates a woman's or girl's fundamental human rights and can have serious consequences in society. For instance, nearly 40 percent of all women who have been murdered worldwide were killed by a husband or dating partner. Overall, violence against women "perpetuates male power and control, either by intention or effect," says Jane Doe Inc. "Violence against women is sustained by a culture of silence and denial of the seriousness of the abuse, its consequences on the personal and social level, and its use as a tool of domination."[23]

> "Violence against women is sustained by a culture of silence and denial of the seriousness of the abuse, its consequences on the personal and social level, and its use as a tool of domination."[23]
> *– Jane Doe Inc., the Massachusetts Coalition Against Sexual Assault and Domestic Violence*

THE VIOLENCE AGAINST WOMEN ACT

When the Violence Against Women Act (VAWA) was passed in 1994 in the United States, its goal was to provide safety, justice, and autonomy to victims of domestic and sexual violence. The original version of the VAWA largely focused on improving how law enforcement and the court system in the United States responded to domestic violence. Not only was the bill designed to improve the criminal justice system with training, resources, and policies, but it also discouraged the idea that domestic violence is a private matter within a relationship. Instead, it emphasized that domestic violence is a crime.

Eventually, it became apparent that domestic and sexual violence issues needed a community response that went beyond what the criminal justice system could provide. As a result, Congress reauthorized the VAWA with revisions that included funding for community support programs. The reauthorizations happened in 2000, 2005, and 2013. Many of the changes from these reauthorizations involved improving services for victims. They specified that sexual assault, dating violence, and stalking are serious crimes that many communities were not prepared to handle. The revisions also called for more legal protections, especially for victims whose race, ethnicity, immigration status, age, disability, sexual orientation, or gender identity make it more difficult to escape domestic violence or pursue justice. In July 2018, Democratic lawmakers proposed another reauthorization of the VAWA.

ROOT CAUSES OF VIOLENCE AGAINST WOMEN

Today's headlines demonstrate that violence against women and girls is a global problem. From domestic violence and murders to acid throwing and honor killings, women around the world are at risk for violence. Violence occurs in every country in the world and impacts people of every race, religion, and socioeconomic class. Statistics show that one in three women will be affected by violence of some type in her lifetime.

While the choice to commit specific acts of violence still lies with the perpetrators of those acts, there are many different factors that contribute to the worldwide prevalence of violence against women. Most experts indicate that absence of gender equality is one of the top reasons for violence against women worldwide. In fact, a 2015 study found that higher levels of inequality correlated with higher levels of domestic violence.

HOW MARRIED DADS REDUCE THE RISK OF VIOLENCE

There are many men who abuse their wives and girlfriends. But there also are men who are more likely to protect women and girls from violence. Many times, these protectors are married biological fathers. Research shows that girls raised in homes with married biological parents are less likely to be assaulted or abused compared with kids who live without their biological dad. According to the report *Fourth National Incidence Study of Child Abuse and Neglect*, "Only 0.7 per 1,000 children living with two married biological parents were sexually abused compared to 12.1 per 1,000 children living with a single parent who had an unmarried partner."

Meanwhile, research from the National Institutes of Health indicates that "Girls who are victimized are . . . more likely to have lived without their natural fathers." This risk for violence is especially high when there is a mother's boyfriend or stepfather in the picture. Another study found that, "Children residing in households of unrelated adults were nearly 50 times as likely to die of injuries [caused by abuse] than children residing with two biological parents."

Researchers suggest that women and girls are safer when their biological parents are married because marriage generally provides stability to the home life. They also say that biological fathers in these homes are more likely to be attentive and engaged with their kids because they expect their marriages to last. This is not to say that married men do not engage in violence, because some do. But for those who do not, being married generally provides an extra level of protection for their wives and children.

Quoted in W. Bradford Wilcox and Robin Fretwell Wilson, "One Way to End Violence Against Women? Married Dads," **Washington Post,** *June 10, 2014.* *www.washingtonpost.com.*

According to the study, women worldwide frequently do not have the same opportunities and rights as men in many areas, including education, employment, and property rights, as well as the freedom to marry and divorce.

Patriarchal views in many societies also contribute to widespread violence against women. Patriarchal views value men as the leaders and decision-makers of society, and they expect women to be submissive. Anytime women are seen as weaker, less important, expendable, or inconvenient, they become viewed as less than human

Violence and domestic abuse can affect women of any race, age, or socioeconomic class. Overall, gender inequality and patriarchal views are believed to contribute to widespread violence against women.

and can be vulnerable to abuse. What's more, patriarchal views create "an environment where women supposedly need men in their life to assert dominance over them, which easily creates a culture of abuse acceptance," said Ashley Easter, an advocate for victims of abuse.[24]

Another issue is the lack of effective laws regarding sexual assault, domestic violence, and other violence against women. For instance, "In many countries, laws against wife assault or sexual assault are lax or non-existent; in many other [countries where laws exist, they] are barely enforced," wrote Michael Kaufman, author of *The Seven P's of Men's Violence*.[25] Meanwhile in other countries, he wrote, the laws are "absurd."[26] For instance, there are countries where rape can only be prosecuted if there are several male witnesses, and the woman's account of what happened is never considered.

> "In many countries, laws against wife assault or sexual assault are lax or non-existent; in many other [countries where laws exist, they] are barely enforced."[25]
> – *Michael Kaufman, author of* The Seven P's of Men's Violence

Personal past experiences also can play a role in violence against women. "Far too many men around the world grew up in households where their mother was beaten by their father," Kaufman wrote. "They grew up seeing violent behaviour towards women as the norm, as just the way life is lived."[27] While some men who witness violence as a child will be determined to never repeat it, others will come to believe it is a normal male response to women. In these cases, violence against women becomes a learned behavior.

> "Far too many men around the world grew up in households where their mother was beaten by their father. They grew up seeing violent behaviour towards women as the norm, as just the way life is lived."[27]
> – *Michael Kaufman, author of* The Seven P's of Men's Violence

Other factors contributing to violence against women include substance abuse, low levels of education, limited economic opportunities, and mental health conditions. Additionally, the UN states that normalizing the use of violence within the family or society to address conflict contributes to the issue as well. Likewise, when communities tolerate male violence and fail to provide safe places for women and girls, they are contributing to violence against women. Even when communities believe in or reinforce female subordination, they are contributing to violence against women.

Overall, violence against women is a complex social, economic, and cultural issue that is influenced by the historical and structural power imbalances between men and women that exist throughout the world in varying degrees. Ultimately, these inequalities can increase a woman's risk for violence, abuse, and exploitation. And until these things are addressed, violence against women will continue to be an issue across the globe.

CHAPTER TWO

WHAT TYPES OF VIOLENCE DO WOMEN FACE?

Being sexually assaulted or raped is a heavy load to carry. Just ask Emma Sulkowicz, a graduate of Columbia University in New York City. After allegedly being raped the first day of her sophomore year in August 2012, Sulkowicz was reluctant to file a complaint. But after learning that other women had had similar experiences, she decided to file a formal complaint with the university in April 2013. Later, she was shocked to learn that her alleged attacker was not going to be kicked out of school despite having three similar complaints against him. In fact, according to the *Columbia Daily Spectator* student newspaper, the university found him "not responsible" for all three allegations.[28] In May 2014, Sulkowicz filed a report with the New York City Police Department. However, police did not pursue charges in the case.

To protest Columbia University's handling of her situation, Sulkowicz decided that she wanted to make a statement about what was happening to not only her but to women on college campuses across the country. As a result, she decided to carry a twin-sized dorm mattress everywhere

Emma Sulkowicz carried a mattress around Columbia University's campus every day as part of her *Carrying the Weight* project, a response to the university's handling of her rape report. Columbia did not discipline the student accused of raping Sulkowicz, who was also a Columbia student.

she went. Her plan was to lug it around until her alleged rapist was kicked off campus. She called it *Carrying the Weight*. She also used the mattress project as part of her senior art thesis project.

Sulkowicz said the idea came to her while working on an art piece at the Yale Norfolk Art Residency. "I had to move a mattress out of a room to make a video," Sulkowicz said. "The image of me moving a mattress got stuck in my head. I think it was because I was raped in my own bed—it was a place associated with a lot of pain and hurt. The idea of me having to carry around my pain everywhere I go was reflected in me bringing the mattress, which is kept in a safe place, out into the light and into

UNIVERSITIES NOT HANDLING SEXUAL ASSAULT PROPERLY

Siding with an alleged perpetrator of sexual violence or brushing a complaint under the rug is not that uncommon among colleges and universities, according to a report in the American Psychological Association journal *Psychology, Public Policy, and Law*. According to lead researcher Corey Rayburn Yung, a law professor at the University of Kansas, the norm is for universities to downplay the situation and the number of incidents.

"Colleges and universities still aren't taking the safety of their students from sexual assault seriously," Yung said. "The study shows that many universities continue to view rape and sexual assault as a public relations issue rather than a safety issue. They don't want to be seen as a school with really high sexual assault numbers, and they don't want to go out of their way to report that information to students or the media."

This lack of intervention can have serious consequences. "The result is students at many universities continue to be attacked and victimized, and punishment isn't meted out to the rapists and sexual assaulters," Yung said.

Quoted in American Psychological Association, "Many Universities Undercount Sexual Assaults on Campus, Research Finds," ScienceDaily, February 2, 2015. www.sciencedaily.com.

the public eye. That mirrored the situation I was in and I felt like it was a good metaphor."[29]

In addition to carrying the mattress every day, Sulkowicz and more than twenty other students filed a federal complaint against Columbia University alleging the school failed to protect victims of sexual assault. Together, the students filed the complaint with the US Department of Education, alleging violations of Title II, Title IX, and the Clery Act. Title II, which is part of the Americans with Disabilities Act, is a civil rights law that prohibits discrimination against people with disabilities in all areas of public life. This includes everything from jobs and schools to transportation. Title IX is part of the Higher Education Act and requires any school receiving money from the US Department of Education to not discriminate based on a person's sex. The Clery Act is a federal law that requires colleges and universities across the country to disclose information about crime on their campuses.

Since Sulkowicz and her classmates filed the federal complaint against Columbia University, the *Columbia Daily Spectator* has reported that the Department of Education's Office of Civil Rights is conducting five investigations into the university's handling of sexual assault cases. This is the highest number of concurrent investigations that the university has ever faced. What's more, with five open investigations, Columbia tied for second for the highest number of active Title IX complaints in the nation, according to reports from the *Chronicle of Higher Education*. "Columbia is more willing to silence and punish survivors and their supporters than serial rapists," the students said in their statement. "Because of this reality, students have decided to file . . . [the complaint] to hold the university accountable for its deliberate mishandling of campus sexual violence and mental health."[30]

Sulkowicz, who carried the mattress until the day she graduated, said the most painful thing for her was dealing with people who didn't believe her. "People somehow [used] the attention I [received] to discredit me," she said. "I know what happened. Why would I lie about something that terrible? That's been the most painful thing—dealing with people who don't believe something that was really traumatic for me."[31]

> "I know what happened. Why would I lie about something that terrible? That's been the most painful thing—dealing with people who don't believe something that was really traumatic for me."[31]
> – *Emma Sulkowicz, rape victim and creator of* Carrying the Weight *project*

In 2016, Sulkowicz received the Woman of Courage Award from the National Association of Women. When she posted about the award on her Instagram account, she took the opportunity to address people who had accused her of not moving on or getting over what happened to her. "Many people ask me how I've 'healed' from my assault, as if healing were another word for 'forgetting about it,' 'getting over it,' or even 'shutting up about it,'" she wrote. "To expect me to move on is to equate courage with self-censorship. The phrases—suck it up, move on, and get over it—are violence."[32]

VIOLENCE AGAINST WOMEN IS COMMON

Sexual assault and rape on college campuses—like what was reported in Sulkowicz's situation—is a huge problem. As many as 25 percent of women (and 15 percent of men) become victims of forced sex while in college. But that is just one facet of violence against women. All across the globe, women are beaten, raped, mutilated, and even murdered at astonishing rates. What's more, violence against women is not limited to a specific culture, region, or country. Every woman and girl in every society is at risk for violence.

Globally, the most common form of violence against women is physical violence that is perpetrated by an intimate partner. For instance, in the United States, one-third of women murdered each year are killed by intimate partners. Meanwhile, the World Health Organization reports that in Israel, Canada, and Australia, 40 to 70 percent of female murder victims were killed by their partners. In South Africa, a woman is killed every six hours, while in Guatemala, two women are murdered on average each day. In fact, there are several worldwide surveys that show half of all women who are murdered are killed by their current or former partners.

Sexual violence is another way in which women are violated. But it is difficult to find consistent statistics because victims of rape and sexual assault often do not report the violence. Women who have been sexually assaulted often feel shame and humiliation, despite the fact that they have done nothing wrong. These feelings stop many victims from reporting what happened. As a result, experts estimate that the statistics for sexual violence are much higher than what they have on record. But even the statistics they do have indicate how prevalent sexual violence is. For instance, in Canada, one study found that 54 percent of girls ages fifteen to nineteen had experienced sexual coercion in dating relationships. Meanwhile, in Switzerland, nearly 23 percent of women experience sexual violence by non-partners in their lifetimes.

Another issue with sexual violence is forced early marriage. More than 60 million girls worldwide are forced to marry before the age of eighteen, especially in South Asia and Sub-Saharan Africa. This practice often leads to young girls and women being victimized. Aside from the abuse they experience at the hands of their spouses and their exposure to sexually transmitted diseases such as HIV/AIDS, they often suffer from fistulas. A fistula is a severe tearing and injury to the vaginal tissues that occurs when a young girl's body is not developmentally ready for sex. When a fistula occurs, girls often become unable to control their urination and defecation. This then makes them socially undesirable, and they are often cast aside, which then leads to additional abuse.

There are also many other problems associated with forced early marriage. For instance, girls who marry before they turn eighteen are less likely to continue their schooling. They also are more likely to give birth to stillborn babies or babies that fail to live past one month. Even worse, child brides are more likely to die due to complications in pregnancy and childbirth than women in their twenties. In fact, 70,000 girls ages fifteen to nineteen die every year due to pregnancy- and childbirth-related issues.

Violence affects women and girls all over the world. This ranges from physical violence to emotional abuse to human trafficking.

And if women and girls live in a country that is at war, they are even more at risk for violence. According to the United Nations, women and girls are often subjected to sexual abuse at the hands of military and rebel forces. For instance, in the Democratic Republic of the Congo, approximately 1,100 rapes are reported each month, with an average of thirty-six women and girls raped every day. Some experts speculate that more than 200,000 women have suffered from sexual violence in that country since the nation's military conflicts began in the late 1990s.

Violence against women can take many different forms, ranging from physical and sexual violence to psychological violence, digital abuse, and economic control. It's common for women to experience multiple forms of violence in the same relationship. Meanwhile, there are some types of violence that are specific to certain cultures or regions such as acid throwing, honor killings, and genital mutilation. And some forms of violence cross national boundaries, such as human trafficking.

PHYSICAL VIOLENCE

Physical violence is probably one of the most recognized forms of violence that women experience. This violence consists of physically aggressive acts such as biting, kicking, punching, slapping, beating, pinching, strangling, and more. Furthermore, these intentionally inflicted injuries are often disguised as accidents both by the perpetrator and the victim. A number of studies indicate that anywhere between 10 percent and 60 percent of women throughout the world have been hit or physically assaulted by a male intimate partner at some point in their lives. Moreover, between 3 percent and 52 percent of women reported physical violence in the previous year. One factor that could explain this difference is the willingness of women to disclose the abuse they are experiencing. What's more, where the violence takes place and how violence is defined by the surrounding community also influence the rates of physical violence reported.

One harrowing example of physical violence is strangulation. Research shows a link between strangulation and the likelihood of domestic homicide. Women who are strangled by a partner are seven times more likely to become the victim of a homicide or attempted homicide by that partner, writes Kate Manne in the *New York Times*. Strangulation also can cause brain damage, throat injuries, and damage to the vocal cords, even when the violence leaves no external bruises or scratches. In fact, half the time strangulation will leave no marks at all, and when it does, only less than half of the marks are dark or appear quickly enough to show up in police photographs.

Physical violence is one of the most easily recognizable forms of violence against women. In a violent relationship, an abuser might hit, kick, or strangle the victim, which can result in injuries or even death.

"[Overall], strangulation sends a powerful message," writes Manne. "What strangulation effectively communicates to a victim, more clearly than words could, is that an abuser is willing to exert punitive control by preying on her most fundamental visceral needs—such as the bodily imperative to gasp for air when she cannot breathe, and the desperate urge to end the intense pain that strangulation causes."[33]

PSYCHOLOGICAL VIOLENCE AND EMOTIONAL VIOLENCE

Emotional violence is one of the most difficult forms of abuse to recognize. Whether it is subtle or overt, it chips away at the victim's self-esteem. Some examples of emotional abuse include calling her names, putting her down, and making her feel guilty. As a result, victims of emotional and psychological abuse begin to doubt their perceptions and reality. When someone is psychologically or emotionally violent, he will control the victim by discrediting, isolating, and silencing her. Some common tactics are humiliation, coercion, threatening, and fear mongering.

Although there is little data available to show how prevalent psychological violence is across countries and cultures, most experts believe that it happens quite often. For instance, 43 percent of women in the twenty-eight European Union member states have experienced some form of psychological violence by an intimate partner in their lifetime.

SEXUAL VIOLENCE

Many people envision a violent attack by a stranger when they think of rape or sexual assault. But the truth is, rape and sexual assault are often perpetrated by someone the victim knows. In fact, the most common perpetrators of sexual violence are intimate partners. What's more, around 120 million girls worldwide have experienced forced intercourse or other forced sexual acts at some point in their lives. More than one in four women in the Washington, DC, area have experienced some form of sexual harassment on public transportation. And 23 percent of female college students have experienced sexual assault or sexual misconduct.

Sexual misconduct is any unwanted sexual activity and can include inappropriate touching, exposing one's own genitals to a victim, or forcing a victim to touch another person. Overall, there is a wide range of acts that fall under the term *sexual violence*. These include rape, unwanted sexual advances and sexual harassment, sexual abuse, forced marriage, denying the use of contraception, and forcing someone to have an abortion.

Although the documented number of women impacted by sexual violence is significant, experts believe the number could actually be much higher. For instance, some research suggests that as many as 67 to 84 percent of sexual violence cases may go unreported, often because of the sensitivity of the issue. For this reason, it is extremely difficult to understand the scope of the problem. What's more, despite the prevalence of sexual violence, most countries have conducted very little research about the issue. Based on the research that is available, it is estimated that nearly one in four women may experience sexual violence by an intimate partner.

ECONOMIC CONTROL

Economic control, also known as financial abuse, involves controlling a victim's ability to obtain, use, and save money. When women are victimized and controlled financially, they may find it hard to make money on their own. For instance, many abusive partners will limit their victim's access to education and forbid them from working. The abusive partner's fear is that any type of financial independence makes it too easy for the victim to leave. If a victim does happen to make her own money, it is often controlled or stolen by the abuser. For instance, she may have to account for every penny she spends or sign her paychecks over to the abuser. Rarely does a victim of abuse have unrestricted access to money and other resources.

Economic control is one of the most powerful ways abusers keep victims trapped in harmful relationships. Many women who experience economic control become so worried about providing for themselves financially that they believe it's easier to endure the abuse rather than end the relationship. What's more, financial abuse can also set up women for other types of abuse, including physical abuse. This is an especially high risk if the victim attempts to earn money on her own, become independent, or leave the relationship, because an abuser may use physical violence to keep that from happening.

DIGITAL DATING ABUSE

For women with access to technology, there is another type of violence known as digital dating abuse. Digital dating abuse occurs when an abusive partner uses technology, including smartphones or social media, to stalk, threaten, harass, or intimidate an intimate partner. One common

Abusers may use text messaging, social media, or emails to harass, threaten, or excessively monitor their partners. This digital dating abuse has started happening with the increased prevalence of technology, such as smartphones.

way abusers use technology to control and manipulate their partners is by sending excessive text messages and expecting an immediate response. Abusers also stalk their partners on social media looking for any indication that they are doing something the abuser considers wrong, such as hanging out with people who the abuser doesn't want the victim to be with. Another way that partners use technology for abuse is by demanding that women send them sexually explicit photos or videos. Or the abusive partner may take the photos and videos without permission. Some abusive partners will even distribute personal photos or videos without consent, especially if they want to humiliate or punish women. Several states have specific laws against distribution of private, sexually explicit photos.

Abusers have also been known to impersonate their partners online and may even go as far as setting up fake social media accounts to spy on their partners. Other digital dating abuse tactics might include demanding passwords to a woman's phone and her social media accounts, excessively checking her social accounts without permission, and using information from her phone or social media to accuse her of wrongdoing. It's also not uncommon for digitally abusive partners to read a partner's text messages and emails to monitor her activity.

GENDER-BASED CHILD ABUSE

In some countries around the world, male children are preferred over girls. As a result, female children may be abused by malnourishment or even infanticide, which is the deliberate killing of a baby shortly after birth. Some families will opt for sex-selective abortions to avoid having a girl. In these situations, the baby's gender is determined with an ultrasound, and if it is discovered that the baby is a girl, the couple will opt for an abortion. In the countries where these practices are common, such as China, Taiwan, South Korea, India, Pakistan, and some Sub-Saharan African countries, the population's female-to-male ratio is much lower than expected.

ACID THROWING

Typically, acid attacks occur because someone wants to ruin a woman's future romantic prospects, her career, and her social status. Consequently, the purpose is usually to disfigure the victim rather than kill her. While the majority of acid attacks occur in developing countries, they are not limited to these areas. In fact, acid throwing is a worldwide phenomenon and has been reported in the United Kingdom, Canada, Italy, and other industrialized countries. Approximately 1,500 acid attacks are recorded worldwide each year, with Bangladesh, India, Pakistan, Nepal, Cambodia, and Uganda having the highest numbers reported. Globally, 80 percent of acid attack victims are women and girls.

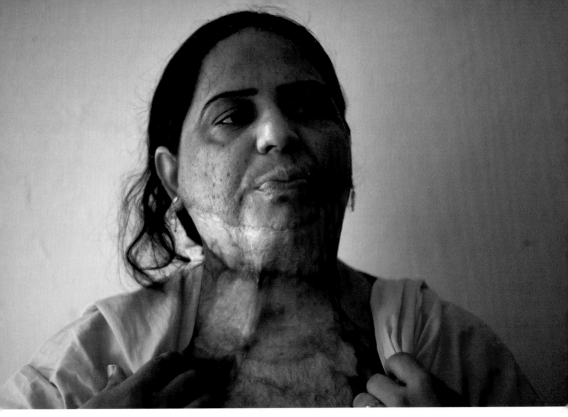

A Pakistani woman shows her scars from suffering an acid attack. A man threw acid at her after her parents rejected a marriage proposal to her.

HONOR KILLINGS

Honor killings are rooted in the belief that a man's honor is linked to the sexual purity of the women in his family. If a woman has sex outside of marriage, certain cultures believe that this disgraces the family's honor and that the only way to cleanse the family is to kill her. Some men will even kill female family members who are raped. When an honor killing occurs, a woman is usually murdered by her brother, father, or another male family member because they believe she brought shame to her family. This type of violence is prevalent in countries in the Eastern Mediterranean region and among some groups in western Europe.

DOWRY MURDER

A dowry is a payment made to a woman's in-laws after she is married. It serves as a gift to her new family. But when a woman's family cannot meet her new family's demands for dowry, she is sometimes killed by her

TYPES OF VIOLENCE
AGAINST WOMEN

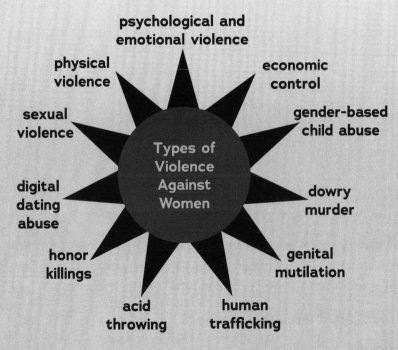

psychological and
emotional violence

physical
violence

economic
control

sexual
violence

gender-based
child abuse

Types of
Violence
Against
Women

digital
dating
abuse

dowry
murder

honor
killings

genital
mutilation

acid
throwing

human
trafficking

Women around the world experience many different types of violence. This
could be in the form of an abusive relationship. In some countries outside the
United States, many women suffer from acid throwing, honor killings, or genital
mutilation. Violence against women can result in injuries, unintended pregnancies,
post-traumatic stress disorder, and even death.

husband or in-laws. Dowries are not common in the United States, but they are often used in other parts of the world. Dowry murder primarily occurs in South Asia. The nations most affected are India, Sri Lanka, Pakistan, and Bangladesh. Aside from murder, the most common forms of dowry-related violence include marital rape, acid throwing, and wife burning. Perpetrators may also starve the victim, deprive her of clothing, and imprison her as a way of extorting money from her family. Violence disguised as a suicide or an accident is also used to punish the women and their families for not meeting the dowry demands.

GENITAL MUTILATION/GENITAL CUTTING

It is estimated that 130 to 140 million women and girls have endured female genital mutilation/genital cutting (FGM/C). Additionally, as many as 3 million girls a year are believed to be at risk for genital mutilation. FGM/C primarily occurs in Africa and in some Middle Eastern countries. In most countries where this happens, the majority of girls are cut before age five. Eighty-five percent of girls in Yemen had experienced FGM/C during the first week of their life, according to a 2016 article in the national *Reproductive Health* journal.

Girls who experience FGM/C are at risk for a number of physical consequences, including excessive bleeding, severe pain, sepsis, and shock. They also may have difficulty urinating or having bowel movements. Although the practice is decreasing, and girls today are about one-third less likely to be cut than thirty years ago, it is still ongoing in many countries. Most communities that practice FGM/C believe that it will ensure a proper marriage for their daughters as well as beauty, chastity, and family honor. Because the practice is such a powerful social norm, many families still have their daughters undergo cutting even when they are aware of the harm it can cause. To them, not performing the procedure would jeopardize not only their daughter's marriage prospects but also the family's status in the community.

HUMAN TRAFFICKING

Just about every country in the world is impacted by human trafficking, which involves taking people against their will and exploiting them in some way. Typically, people who are trafficked are forced into sex or work. While both men and women may become victims of human trafficking, women and girls are most often the ones being victimized. Although it is difficult to quantify how many people are trafficked each year, some estimate that as many as 2.5 million people are trafficked annually into prostitution, forced labor, and more. Approximately 80 percent of these victims are women and girls.

Because women are often more impacted by poverty and discrimination than men, traffickers tend to target them and exploit their vulnerabilities. Perhaps the biggest risk factor for human trafficking is a desperate economic situation. When women try to find jobs, get work permits, or apply for visas or other travel documents, traffickers lure them into their network with lies and false promises. For example, women who apply for jobs abroad as nannies, dancers, and waitresses later find that these are not legitimate positions and are instead held against their will and forced into prostitution. Women who are trafficked also are often subjected to physical violence, sexual assault and rape, imprisonment, and other types of coercion.

WHY DON'T VICTIMS LEAVE VIOLENT RELATIONSHIPS?

Regarding domestic abuse and abusive relationships, one of the first things people often ask about the victims is: "Why doesn't she just leave?" It is rarely that simple. The truth is that leaving an abusive relationship is often the most dangerous time for the victim. Because abuse is about having power and control over a victim, when she leaves, she is taking away the control the perpetrator has over her and threatening his power. As a result, this often causes the violent person to retaliate in very

99%
OF VICTIMS ARE
NEVER
RESCUED

HUMAN
TRAFFICKING
IS THE
FASTEST
GROWING
CRIME

2 MILLION
CHILDREN
ARE EXPLOITED INTO THE
SEX TRADE EACH YEAR

Human trafficking is a worldwide problem. People in many countries, such as this group in England, have organized protests and rallies to raise awareness.

destructive ways in order to regain his power and his control. In fact, the risk of death or injury increases substantially when the victim flees.

There are a number of other reasons that might keep a person from leaving an abusive relationship. Aside from the fear that often keeps victims rooted in their situations, many abused women believe that the violence they are experiencing is normal. Maybe she grew up in a home that was violent. Or perhaps violence against women is a normal part of her culture or environment. Many women do not realize that the abuse they are enduring is unacceptable.

Many times, victims of violence still love their partner—even though that partner is abusive. They also may have children together, and the person who is being abused wants to do what she can to maintain

WHAT DOES DATING VIOLENCE LOOK LIKE?

Identifying dating violence is not as easy as it sounds. "Dating violence doesn't have an age restriction. It isn't defined by gender identity. And it doesn't look the same for every relationship," said Brian Pinero, vice president of victim services at the Rape, Abuse & Incest National Network (RAINN). "The answer to the question, 'What does dating violence look like?' isn't so straightforward—and that's what can make it difficult to spot."

But learning how to spot the early warning signs can provide an opportunity for people at risk to exit a relationship safely before they are hurt further. Dating violence can include everything from physical and emotional abuse to name-calling and even sexual violence, but a commonality in nearly all abusive relationships is that the abuser has power and control over the victim. The abuse is usually not physically violent right away. Early on, the abuse often consists of subtle controlling behaviors such as extreme jealousy, demanding to know where someone is at all times, or controlling the clothing a person wears. Other warning signs include checking cell phone messages, emails, and social media without permission; belittling someone or putting her down; isolating someone from her family and friends; and repeatedly pressuring someone to have sex.

Being abused is scary, and it is important for victims to realize that they are not alone. There are people out there who are ready and willing to help. The National Domestic Violence Hotline (1-800-799-SAFE) is available for anyone experiencing abuse. Teens can text "loveis" to 22522 for support and information. For those who have experienced sexual assault, the National Sexual Assault Hotline (1-800-656-HOPE) is available.

Quoted in "Early Warning Signs of Dating Violence," RAINN, February 6, 2017.
www.rainn.org.

the family. What's more, violent people also can be charming, and the victim may hope that her partner will become the person whom she loves again, especially if she just tries harder. In these cases, the victim wants the violence to stop but does not want the relationship to end.

Shame and embarrassment are two other issues that keep people from acknowledging that they have been abused. Victims also may feel as if they have done something wrong or that they are to blame in some way. Additionally, they may worry that their friends and family will judge them. Another factor keeping women from leaving violent relationships is low self-esteem. When a violent person constantly beats his partner or humiliates her, it can be easy for the victim to believe that she deserves the treatment she is receiving.

Immigration status and language barriers also keep people from reporting violence or trying to leave an unhealthy situation. For instance, in the United States, an undocumented immigrant may fear that reporting violence will affect her immigration status. Additionally, if her first language isn't English, it can be difficult to communicate to others what is happening to her.

A person who is disabled or handicapped may also find it exceptionally difficult to leave a violent situation. She may feel physically dependent on the violent person and feel that her well-being is connected to the relationship. These feelings can heavily influence her decisions to stay. Additionally, if the woman is financially dependent on her partner, she may see no way out. Without money, access to resources, or even a place to go, it can seem impossible for a woman to ever leave an abusive relationship.

Finally, many women stay in violent situations because of cultural or religious beliefs. For instance, traditional gender roles influence them to stay. They fear leaving may bring shame to themselves or their families. Many women also will stay in a violent situation if they have children and fear that they would lose custody or never see the children again if they left.

Overall, violence against women is a significant human rights issue. Left unaddressed, it impacts the health, dignity, and security of its victims. It also takes a toll on the world as a whole and impacts the contributions that women and girls can make to the world around them.

CHAPTER THREE

WHAT ARE THE EFFECTS OF VIOLENCE AGAINST WOMEN?

||||

Judy Malinowski was a beautiful young woman with a bright future ahead of her. The former New Albany, Ohio, beauty queen had survived ovarian cancer and an opioid addiction, and she was focused on raising her two young daughters. But, like many young women, she became involved with a man who did not have her best interests in mind. Her boyfriend, Michael Slager, was mean, controlling, and violent.

Although Malinowski tried to put distance between herself and Slager, he regularly threatened and stalked her. Then, one night in August 2015, the violence escalated. Following an argument behind a gas station in Gahanna, Ohio, Slager doused Malinowski with gasoline and set her on fire using a cigarette lighter. Witnesses called 911 saying that a woman was engulfed in flames and that she had been set on fire by a man later identified as Slager.

The scene was gruesome as bystanders stared in disbelief. "Witness accounts read like something from a horror movie," reported 10TV, a television station in Columbus, Ohio.[34] The reports included statements like "she was completely on fire," and "staggering around in the grass."[35]

Malinowski remembered that night vividly and shared her memories with John Dauphin, a freelance writer and family friend: "I [was] engulfed in flames, and trying to get the fire out of my face. . . . I remember screaming for [Slager] to help me. He was looking at me with this look, and it was so evil. It was the worst look I have ever seen."[36] Malinowski told another TV station, "I never knew that a human being could be so evil. He just stood there and did nothing. The look in his eyes was pure evil."[37]

The attack left Malinowski fighting for her life. Ninety percent of her body was covered in third- and fourth-degree burns. When

> "I remember screaming. . . . He was looking at me with this look, and it was so evil. It was the worst look I have ever seen."[36]
> – Judy Malinowski, victim of domestic violence

doctors reached out to Malinowski's mother, Bonnie Bowes, they warned her that she might not recognize her own daughter. And they were right.

"[She] just didn't even look like a human being," Bowes said. "[But] all I could see was my baby in that bed. All I could see was that she was alive."[38] Hospitalized in Ohio State University's Wexner Medical Center in critical condition, that first night was just the beginning of Malinowski's fight. She would endure more than fifty surgeries and eight months of unconsciousness.

Meanwhile, Slager maintained that the fire was an accident. He claimed he was trying to light a cigarette when Malinowski caught fire. But investigators say security cameras caught Slager dousing her in gasoline and then setting her on fire.

Eventually, forty-one-year-old Slager was sentenced to eleven years in prison. He was convicted of aggravated arson, possession of criminal tools, and assault. Eleven years was the maximum sentence possible at the time for Slager's crimes. But shortly after Malinowski's story became known, Ohio lawmakers began working on legislation known as Judy's Law that would increase penalties for attacks that left women disfigured.

Malinowski clung to life for nearly two years. Her hope was that women everywhere would hear her story and learn from it. But eventually, at age thirty-three, Malinowski succumbed to her injuries and passed away. Slager was charged with murder in connection with her death. Before Malinowski died, she took steps to ensure that her voice would continue to be heard. She provided a video testimony that would have been used in Slager's murder trial. However, in July 2018, just one day before jury selection in Slager's trial, he pleaded guilty in exchange for having the death penalty removed as a possible punishment. He was sentenced to spend the rest of his life in prison without the possibility of parole.

According to Malinowski's mother, a life sentence is what Malinowski would have wanted. In fact, in the video, Malinowski says that she does not want to see Slager executed for her murder. But Malinowski and her mother did want to see Slager admit to his crimes. "You can't fathom what (it's like with) 90 percent of your body with third and fourth degree (burns) and face your attacker and relive that day," said Bowes, Malinowski's mother. "I could not accept anything but a guilty plea because for 700 days Judy's story never, ever wavered in what happened."[39]

PAYING THE ULTIMATE PRICE

As difficult as it is to imagine, stories like Malinowski's are not that uncommon. Every day, approximately three women are murdered in the United States by current or former partners, according to the Violence Policy Center. And worldwide, it is estimated that of all women who were homicide victims in 2012, nearly half were killed by intimate partners or

A CLOSER LOOK AT JUDY'S LAW

The day after her death in June 2017, Judy Malinowski was honored with a moment of silence by the full Ohio Senate chamber. Then the senators unanimously passed legislation that added an additional six years to the maximum prison sentence for assaults involving an accelerant (such as gasoline) that left victims permanently disfigured or incapacitated. The legislation, called Judy's Law, is aimed at preventing future attacks like what Malinowski endured. Lawmakers pursued the legislation because they were inspired by Malinowski's story and appalled by the fact that her attacker was sentenced to just eleven years in prison. State Rep. Jim Hughes, a Republican from Upper Arlington, sponsored the legislation.

"[Malinowski] was a very brave and courageous lady, and inspiration for her family and for everybody," Hughes recalled. The first time he met her, he said, Malinowski declined to take her pain medication "so that she could be her sharpest, at her best, to explain why this legislation was so important. That's a living legacy she's leaving to everyone."

Three months after Malinowski's death, in September 2017, Ohio Governor John Kasich formally signed Judy's Law with Malinowski's two daughters standing at his side. He also vowed to look at existing domestic violence laws to see if they are comprehensive enough to protect women from violence.

Quoted in Rita Price, "Burned Woman Who Inspired Legislation Dies at 33," Columbus Dispatch, June 27, 2017. www.dispatch.com.

family members. Less than 6 percent of male homicide victims were killed by intimate partners in the same year.

For women in abusive relationships, the highest risk of death often comes when attempting to leave the relationship, as was the case with Malinowski. Seventy-five percent of domestic violence homicides occur once the couple is separated. There is a 75 percent increase in violence for at least two years after the separation. "Research has shown the risk of domestic homicide becomes highest during the period of separation," said Betty Jo Barrett, an intimate-partner violence researcher and women's and gender studies professor at the University of Windsor. "And the intensity of domestic violence escalates when the abused person decides to leave the relationship."[40]

Many times, even if women successfully leave a violent situation, the abusers can track them down. For example, some men locate their victims through GPS locators on their phones. Other men will diligently call every shelter in the city or fill out a missing persons report to track down their fleeing partners. Leaving a violent relationship is very different from ending a non-abusive relationship. The endings of violent relationships are fraught with risks that put women in danger of paying the ultimate price.

"Research has shown the risk of domestic homicide becomes highest during the period of separation. And the intensity of domestic violence escalates when the abused person decides to leave the relationship."[40]
– Betty Jo Barrett, domestic violence researcher

Many abuse victims experience long-term physical and mental health issues. The abuse can also affect victims' economic stability. Additionally, the violence and abuse inflicted on women affects their children, families, and communities.

PHYSICAL HEALTH EFFECTS

Violence against women has a direct impact on physical health. Although an abuser may push or shove a victim without causing injury, many instances of domestic violence result in physical injuries, from bruises to broken bones. The World Health Organization (WHO) estimates that roughly 40 percent of all female victims of intimate-partner violence are injured in the process. Meanwhile, in the United States, experts estimate that half of all women who are victims of domestic violence are physically injured by an intimate partner. The most common non-fatal injuries are to the head, neck, or face, followed by musculoskeletal and genital injuries. Aside from these immediate injuries from the abuse, women also may suffer from chronic pain, gastrointestinal disorders, sleep issues,

BLACK WOMEN ARE MORE LIKELY TO DIE IN DOMESTIC VIOLENCE THAN WHITE WOMEN

Domestic violence risks are especially high for black women. In fact, they are almost three times as likely to die as a result of domestic violence than white women. They also are 30 to 50 percent more likely to experience domestic violence than white women. Yet, as domestic violence is an underreported crime, these victims' first response is often to not report the violence.

"Black women tend to feel obligated to put racial issues ahead of sex-based issues. For Black women, a strong sense of cultural affinity and loyalty to community and race renders many of us silent, so our stories often go untold," activist Feminista Jones wrote in *Time* magazine. "One of the biggest related impediments is our hesitation in trusting the police or the justice system. As Black people, we don't always feel comfortable surrendering 'our own' to the treatment of a racially biased police state and as women, we don't always feel safe calling police officers who may harm us instead of helping us."[1]

Black women also generally feel they need to be strong and that asking for help would be a sign of weakness, says Zoë Flowers, an advocate that has spent 17 years in the field of domestic violence. "This idea of strong black women is rewarded and is something that can even be a source of resilience. But it can also leave us feeling like we have no one to turn to," Flowers said.[2]

1. Quoted in Feminista Jones, "Why Black Women Struggle More with Domestic Violence," Time, September 10, 2014. www.time.com.
2. Quoted in "Black Women Are Staying Silent," Domesticshelters.org, April 9, 2018. www.domesticshelters.org.

eating disorders, reproductive health problems, irregular heartbeats, and much more.

Domestic violence can also be fatal. One tactic used by violent men is strangulation. Strangulation rarely leaves striking or vivid marks and bruises, which can make people underestimate the seriousness of the issue. In some cases, this means the victims don't receive the medical attention they need. In fact, injuries "may appear mild initially but they can result in a victim's death within 36 hours," according to Stop Violence Against Women, a human rights advocacy group.[41] Even if strangulation doesn't cause a woman's death, it increases the risk that she will eventually die at the hands of the abuser. For example, a study in the *Journal of Emergency Medicine* discovered that nearly half of all women murdered by a partner had been strangled. Likewise, 45 percent of women who were victims of attempted murder by an intimate partner had been strangled by that partner in the past year.

Marriage is often believed to grant men unconditional sex with their wives, and marital rape is not against the law in many countries. Because of this, many men around the world feel they have permission to use violence if their wives do not comply with their sexual requests. This sexual violence puts women at an increased risk of unplanned pregnancies, as well as sexually transmitted diseases such as HIV/AIDS.

Women are particularly vulnerable to violent attacks when they are pregnant. As a result, many abused women experience medical difficulties with their pregnancies. A US study found that women who experience violence at the hands of a partner are three times more likely to have reproductive health problems than non-abused women. Women who are victims of sexual violence also are more likely to have a history of sexually transmitted diseases, vaginal and cervical infections, kidney infections, and bleeding during pregnancy. What's more, abused women are more likely to delay prenatal care and are less likely to see a medical professional during their pregnancy. "Intimate partner abuse during pregnancy may be a more significant factor for pregnancy complications than other conditions for which pregnant women are routinely screened, such as hypertension and diabetes," says Stop Violence Against Women.[42]

Meanwhile, according to the UN Population Fund, "222 million women in developing countries today do not have the means to delay pregnancies and childbearing."[43] This is in part due to coercion, violence, and even marital rape by an intimate partner. And research presented at the 2010 International AIDS Conference indicates that the risk of contracting HIV

Pregnant women are particularly vulnerable to abuse. Any abuse to a pregnant woman will likely hurt her child as well.

is at least two times greater for women who are victimized by violence. Additionally, the WHO reports that women who are victims of domestic violence are more likely to report having had an abortion against their will. To make matters worse, forced abortions tend to be underreported and often take place in unsafe conditions. When this happens, it places a woman's health at an even greater risk.

MENTAL HEALTH EFFECTS

Immediately following a violent incident, it is not uncommon for women who are abused to feel fear, anger, and confusion. They also may feel guilty or ashamed for being assaulted. Many victims of violence try to hide the abuse by covering bruises with long sleeves or makeup. They may even make excuses for the abuser. Some women report feeling numb or not feeling anything at all.

As the abuse continues, these initial feelings can manifest into serious, long-term mental health conditions. For instance, women who are victimized by violence may experience post-traumatic stress disorder (PTSD), depression, anxiety, panic attacks, and more. They also have a high risk of developing schizophrenia-like psychotic symptoms. This risk is doubled for women who were also victims of childhood abuse. Other mental health effects that women may experience include not wanting to do things that they once enjoyed, shutting people out, not being able to trust others, and having low self-esteem.

PTSD is a mental health disorder that occurs in people who have witnessed or have experienced a traumatic event such as combat, a car accident, a natural disaster, physical violence, or sexual assault. Victims of violence who develop PTSD may startle easily, feel tense or on edge, have difficulty sleeping, or have angry outbursts. They also may have trouble remembering things or have negative thoughts about themselves and others. Fifty-four to 84 percent of battered women suffer from PTSD, according to the Florida Coalition Against Domestic Violence (FCADV). Sixty-three to 77 percent of battered women experience depression, and 38 to 75 percent suffer from anxiety, according to the FCADV.

Many victims of violence cope with this trauma by using drugs, drinking alcohol, smoking, or overeating. Substance abuse has been found to occur in 40 to 60 percent of domestic violence situations, according to the American Society of Addiction Medicine. Likewise, women in violent relationships often report being coerced by their partners into using alcohol or drugs. When it is the abusive partner who uses drugs or alcohol, research has found that physical violence is eleven times more likely to happen at times when the abuser is using those substances.

Finally, women who are abused may be more likely to commit suicide. For instance, the United Nations Children's Fund (UNICEF) reported that a "close correlation between domestic violence and suicide has been established based on studies in the United States, Fiji, Papua New Guinea, Peru, India, Bangladesh, and Sri Lanka."[44] The organization also found that "suicide is 12 times as likely to have been attempted by a woman who has been abused than by one who has not."[45] Louise Arseneault, a researcher at the Institute of Psychiatry, Psychology & Neuroscience at King's College London, said:

> Domestic violence is unacceptable because of the injuries it causes. We have shown that these injuries are not only physical: they can also be psychological, as they increase the risk of depression and psychotic symptoms. Health professionals need to be very aware of the possibility that women who experience mental health problems may also be the victims of domestic violence. . . . Given the prevalence of depression in these victims, we need to prevent these situations and take action. These acts of violence do more than leave physical damage; they leave psychological scars as well.[46]

EFFECTS ON WORK

Aside from the numerous physical and mental health effects, violence against women can also affect them in many other ways. For instance,

"Given the prevalence of depression in [domestic violence] victims, we need to prevent these situations and take action. These acts of violence do more than leave physical damage; they leave psychological scars as well."[46]
– Louise Arseneault, researcher at King's College London

53

Abusive relationships affect victims' careers. The abuse may make a woman stressed at work, or she may even be unable to go to work because of injuries or a controlling partner.

experiencing violence or sexual trauma can interfere with a woman's ability to work. The US Department of Health and Human Services reports that half of women who experience sexual assault have had to quit their jobs or were forced to leave their jobs in the first year after the assault. As a result, these women reportedly lose nearly $250,000 each during their lifetimes. Research also shows that women who experience intimate-partner violence often have casual and part-time work, instead of full-time work, and earn 60 percent less than women who do not experience violence. Women's careers can also be affected if they have to miss work due to injuries inflicted by domestic violence or due to a controlling partner. Studies in India show that women can lose an average of at least five paid work days for each incident of intimate-partner violence. And in Uganda, about 9 percent of violent incidents forced women to lose time from work. This totaled approximately eleven days a year for each woman, which is equivalent to half a month's salary. When situations like this occur, the woman is not the only person affected. Her children and any other people dependent on her income are impacted as well.

HOMELESSNESS

Homelessness is another issue closely tied to violence against women. A 2017 report by the DC Interagency Council on Homelessness found that 31 percent, or nearly one third, of the women they interviewed in the Washington, DC, area said that they are homeless because of the past violence they have experienced. The report also found that approximately 25 percent of the women surveyed did not stay in any kind of shelter when fleeing their violent situation. "About 12 percent said they had spent most of the past month on the streets, and another 12 percent were 'unstably housed,' often couch-surfing in people's homes," according to the *Washington Post*.[47] Without a safe place to stay, they were at risk for more violence.

For example, 54 percent of these women said they have experienced violence while homeless. And if the woman had experienced violence in the past, she was even more likely to experience it on the streets, with 63 percent of women who had been abused in the past experiencing violence while homeless. What's more, 28 percent of women said they had been at some time during their homelessness forced, threatened, or pressured into having sex. Meanwhile, 29 percent of the homeless women interviewed said they had engaged in what is known as "survival sex." In other words, they traded sex for money, food, alcohol, drugs, or a place to stay. "Abuse affects a person's self-esteem or sense of worth. People can become less careful about putting themselves in dangerous situations," said Schroeder Stribling, executive director of N Street Village, the largest service provider for homeless women in Washington, DC. "They lose some of their own internal alarm system."[48]

> "Abuse affects a person's self-esteem or sense of worth. People can become less careful about putting themselves in dangerous situations."[48]
> – Schroeder Stribling, executive director of a nonprofit for homeless women

ECONOMIC IMPACT

The costs of addressing violence against women are extremely high and have a significant economic impact on the world at large. These costs include the direct costs of services to treat and support abused women and their children, as well as the costs to bring perpetrators to justice. "Annual costs of intimate partner violence have been calculated at $5.8 billion in the United States and $1.16 billion in Canada," according to Lakshmi Puri, UN assistant secretary-general and deputy executive director of UN Women.[49] Overall, "Research indicates that the cost of violence against women . . . is equivalent to $1.5 trillion," Puri said. "Further, research findings reveal that domestic and intimate partner violence cause more deaths and entail much higher economic costs than homicides or civil wars."[50]

The cost of services is significant. In the United States, the cost of intimate-partner violence is $4.1 billion for medical and health care services. Puri said, "Violence against women and girls brings economic costs to any society. The negative impact on women's participation in education, employment and civic life undermines poverty reduction.

It results in lost employment and productivity, and it drains resources from social services, the justice system, health-care agencies and employers."[51] As violence against women affects not only women themselves but also society as a whole, experts say people must work together to stop this violence from happening. Violence against women is not a problem for just victims to solve, and it's not a problem for only women to solve. Government leaders and community members must come together to address this issue, and there is still a lot of work to be done.

"Violence against women and girls brings economic costs to any society. The negative impact on women's participation in education, employment and civic life undermines poverty reduction. It results in lost employment and productivity, and it drains resources from social services, the justice system, health-care agencies and employers."[51]
– Lakshmi Puri, UN assistant secretary-general and deputy executive director of UN Women

CHAPTER FOUR

HOW CAN VIOLENCE AGAINST WOMEN BE PREVENTED?

IIII

In 2006, Tarana Burke, a women's advocate in New York, coined the phrase "Me Too" as a way to empower women who had survived sexual violence, especially young women of color from low-income communities. More than a decade later, the phrase was reintroduced by actress Alyssa Milano on Twitter as a hashtag, #MeToo. Milano's goal was to empower people to openly acknowledge their experiences as victims of sexual violence and sexual harassment. The response was significant, resulting in a national movement and eventually exposing the sexually violent actions of many high-profile, powerful men.

Milano's use of #MeToo was prompted by a *New York Times* article accusing Harvey Weinstein, a famous Hollywood producer, of sexual harassment. Actresses Rose McGowan and Ashley Judd were among Weinstein's accusers. After the article, Milano wanted #MeToo to keep the conversation going by raising awareness of the prevalence of sexual harassment. As a result, the words "Me Too" were tweeted, posted, and written about more than 12 million times over the next few weeks.

The phrase "Me Too" has become a rallying cry for modern feminists, especially to raise awareness of sexual harassment and sexual assault. The phrase was introduced by activist Tarana Burke and then popularized into a hashtag by actress Alyssa Milano.

Women all over the country were using the hashtag, often accompanied by stories about the harassment or abuse they had experienced. The hashtag became the national #MeToo movement, shedding light on an issue that people often didn't talk about. The movement empowered more women to come forward with revelations about Weinstein's conduct. Some of what he is accused of includes forcing women to massage him and watch him naked. He also is accused of sexual assault and promising to advance acting careers in return for sexual favors. Weinstein was arrested in 2018 as a result of these allegations. Amid the Weinstein case and the popularization of #MeToo, many other high-profile men—including actors, politicians, and TV news personalities—were also accused of sexual harassment.

One of the most notable accomplishments of the #MeToo movement, though, is the fact that it has diminished much of the unnecessary shame and humiliation associated with victims of sexual assault by letting these victims know that they are not alone in their experiences. The movement has taken away the sense of isolation that many sexual violence survivors feel, and it has given them a community of support. It has also provided a platform where women feel safe sharing their stories without fear. The movement also has the country talking openly about this uncomfortable, but very real, issue.

A CLOSER LOOK AT THE UNITED STATES

Efforts like #MeToo and legislation like the Violence Against Women Act (VAWA) have helped the United States make strides toward stopping violence against women. While most advocates would say that the country still has a long way to go, there have been some improvements along the way. For instance, a report from the Bureau of Justice Statistics indicates that the rate of sexual violence against women and girls age twelve and older fell by 64 percent between 1995 and 2005, but it remained stable in the five years since 2005. According to the report, women and girls in the United States endured approximately 270,000 rapes or sexual assaults in 2010, compared with 556,000 in 1995. Eleanor Smeal, president of the Feminist Majority, a national nonprofit, said, "The new study is proof that the newly reauthorized Violence Against Women

Act and awareness of the problem by police is having a positive impact."[52] Smeal and her organization have been working to reduce how frequently violence against women occurs.

The report also indicated that although most authorities feel reporting rape and sexual assaults to police is an important way to stop those crimes from happening, reporting trends have been uneven. For instance, an estimated 29 percent of rapes and sexual assaults were reported to police in 1995. By 2003, the rate of reporting had increased to 56 percent. But by 2010, it had declined to only 35 percent. Meanwhile, of the 283,200 rapes or sexual assaults reported on average in a year, only 12 percent resulted in arrest during the time period between 2005 and 2010. "Everybody knows that rape and sexual assault are crimes and will be treated as such," Smeal said. "[But], we have a ways to go. It is clear there is still too much violence and too many are fearful to report it."[53]

However, there are many times when victims find the courage and come forward to report a crime only to realize that the police can't or won't do anything about it. Mary P. Koss, a professor of public health at the University of Arizona, said

> "Everybody knows that rape and sexual assault are crimes and will be treated as such. [But], we have a ways to go. It is clear there is still too much violence and too many are fearful to report it."[53]
> – Eleanor Smeal, president of the Feminist Majority

the fact that only 12 percent of perpetrators are arrested "should puncture the public's illusion that rape victims can achieve justice through reporting to law enforcement."[54] Meanwhile, when people see that very few reports result in an arrest, they often assume that it's because the women filed false reports or that an assault never happened. But, according to Koss, that is an incorrect assumption. The number of false reports is actually very small, she said, ranging from 2 to 4 percent.

STRATEGIES FOR ADDRESSING VIOLENCE AGAINST WOMEN

Although patterns of violence against women vary in some ways between different countries, the UN has outlined what it believes are the most important components of addressing violence against women worldwide. Not every country has put these core components in place, but the UN is making progress in educating countries about how to address violence against women.

Among these strategies is the suggestion that countries develop comprehensive laws addressing violence against women that allow for perpetrators to be prosecuted and victims to be supported. The UN also suggests that countries create laws that give women equal rights when it comes to marriage, divorce, property ownership, and custody of children. By giving women more independence, these types of laws could help them leave violent relationships.

Countries should also strive to provide victims of violence immediate protection and support including medical treatment, police interventions, legal assistance, and safe accommodations, the UN suggests. This could be facilitated by implementing training programs for law enforcement, health-care workers, social workers, and members of the judicial system to ensure they know how to address situations involving violence against women. It would also help for countries to develop prevention programs that give women better access to education, employment, politics, and leisure activities. Violence prevention programs should be integrated with other programs, such as those addressing poverty, housing, and education, to ensure that the issues that make women more vulnerable to violence are being addressed, according to the UN. The UN also suggests that countries collect data on the magnitude, causes, and consequences of violence against women and analyze it based on age,

GLOBAL STRATEGIES TO REDUCE VIOLENCE

The Global Violence Reduction Conference, led by the World Health Organization (WHO) and the University of Cambridge, aimed to develop strategies and goals for reducing violence worldwide. It brought together 150 representatives from international organizations, academic settings, and philanthropic organizations to discuss how violence can be reduced globally. At the center of their discussions was the question: "Is it possible to cut worldwide levels of interpersonal violence in half within the coming 30 years?" They concluded in a 2015 report that this goal in question could be achieved if policymakers harness the power of scientific evidence on violence reduction.

With this goal, the world's current homicide rate of 6.4 per 100,000 people could be halved by 2045. While homicides are among the best-documented indicators of global violence decline, the representatives at this conference also intended to address other forms of violence such as sexual violence and violence against women. To do this, conference participants developed several strategies. For instance, one of their goals is to protect the most vulnerable people in the world from violence, which includes women, children, and teens. They also feel that they need to focus their efforts on addressing violence in low- and middle-income countries, along with the world's most violent cities. "Overall there is a strong . . . case for the possibility of [violence reduction]," said Harvard professor Steven Pinker. For instance, countries have become better not only at providing justice but also at cooperating and working together to uphold human rights while putting an end to justifications for violence.

Quoted in World Health Organization and University of Cambridge, "Global Strategies to Reduce Violence by 50% in 30 Years," University of Cambridge, Institute of Criminology, Violence Research Centre, *April 2015. p. 22.*

ethnicity, disability, place of occurrence, and other relevant characteristics. This information will serve as a basis for laws, policies, and programs.

HOW MEN CAN HELP

Violence against women is more than a women's issue. It is a men's issue too. After all, no one wants good men taking the blame for what only some men choose to do. But, more importantly, no person—man or woman—should feel that it is acceptable for other people to be abused. Violence will end more quickly when men step up and help create a culture in which violence against women is unacceptable, according to a

White Ribbon Foundation report. This Australian foundation encourages men to step up and walk beside women to help create a culture in which violence does not exist.

When men get involved in efforts to end violence, it means that women do not have to make the change alone. But not only are women and girls benefitting from these efforts—men are, too. After all, violence against women hurts the world's communities, especially when men are witnesses to violence against women and yet do nothing. But when men challenge violent behaviors, they also are challenging gender inequality and oppression. "Non-abusive men may not realize it but they have the potential to make an enormous difference in helping to stop domestic violence and sexual assault," according to the Domestic Violence Prevention Centre in Australia.[55]

"Non-abusive men may not realize it but they have the potential to make an enormous difference in helping to stop domestic violence and sexual assault."[55]
– Domestic Violence Prevention Centre in Australia

There are several things men can do to help. For instance, they can be positive role models for other men. They should encourage other men to also be aware of violence against women. And when they do see violence, they should step up and say something. Another way men can help is to understand how their own attitudes, actions, and words may be perpetuating violence against women without them even knowing it. For example, this happens when men tell sexist jokes or purchase magazines or movies that objectify women or promote violence against women.

HOW INDIVIDUAL PEOPLE CAN HELP END VIOLENCE AGAINST WOMEN

Everyone has a responsibility to help end violence against women and girls. But not everyone knows what to do. For this reason, organizations like UN Women have come up with ways in which the average person can help promote the safety of women and girls. The first step is telling people that violence against women and girls is never acceptable. Do not support music, movies, and other media that glorify violence against women. And if people see violence or harassment happening, they should say something or do something about it.

For instance, if people see a friend, classmate, or teammate being disrespectful or abusing a woman or a girl, they should find a way to say something about the disrespectful or abusive behavior. Remember that if people are silent about abuse, the abuse will continue.

Another point to remember is that words are powerful and can easily hurt other people. People should strive to be respectful and caring in any relationship. For example, if someone is angry about something his partner did or said, he can calm himself by counting to ten before reacting. That technique may not work for everyone, though, so people should come up with their own ways to make sure their behavior remains respectful. People should not use violence to solve problems.

Another way to help end violence against women is to believe women who say that they have been sexually assaulted, raped, beaten, or abused. It shouldn't matter what a woman was wearing or what she did or said before the abuse—no one ever deserves to be assaulted or abused. And, if people suspect that a woman they know is experiencing violence, they should listen to her and support her. They should also remind her that there are people out there who want to help. They can help her find resources such as counselors, shelters, and domestic violence hotlines.

People can also learn more about the overall issue of violence against women and girls, and then they can talk to family members and friends about the problems and how to support one another. People can help by volunteering to work with programs that focus on preventing violence against women and girls.

While friends and family members can support a domestic violence victim, these victims must be allowed to make major decisions for themselves. Each situation is different, and each victim knows what's best for herself.

HOW TO END PERSONAL VIOLENCE

For girls and women who are experiencing domestic violence themselves, there are no quick fixes, but there are ways to get help. First, a person who is being abused can learn about the patterns of abuse. This includes learning to recognize the first signs of abuse, identifying the cycle of abuse, and discovering different techniques for staying safe. Once equipped with this information, she can plan a course of action. However, every relationship is different, so every plan of action will be different as well.

The first step to ending abuse is being able to recognize it and name it. Too many times, victims of violence do not realize that the words or actions of an abuser are considered abusive. Once a woman learns how to spot abuse, she can stop blaming herself for another person's actions. It's also important for abuse victims to recognize that they can't change or help their abuser; they need to help themselves. Each situation is very different, but some options for help may be to call police, call a domestic violence hotline or shelter, or end the abusive relationship.

Another important aspect when dealing with violent and abusive behavior is for victims to recognize that they have value and worth. This generally is not easy for someone who has suffered abuse. The first step in accomplishing this is to remember that abuse steals a person's self-confidence because the actions and words of an abuser are usually packed with lies, including lies about the victim's self-worth. Consequently, victims of violence need to reject those lies and replace them with the truth. It's also important to learn how to set boundaries in relationships. Setting boundaries will guard victims against allowing others to take control.

If possible, violence should not be handled alone. It is important that victims are encouraged to seek professional help and support for their situation. They can contact a local support group or find a counselor who will guide them through the process of dealing with a violent situation. It's also important for victims to surround themselves with people who love and support them. They need people in their lives who will not pressure them to make decisions, such as a decision to leave an abusive relationship, before they are ready. Instead, supportive people should

It's important for friends, family members, and others to listen to victims of violence and to believe their stories. It can be difficult for people to know how to help, but there are many professional resources available.

empower victims to make decisions of their own accord, when they are ready to do so. Each person's situation is different. At the core, each domestic abuse victim knows what is best for herself.

AN ONGOING PROBLEM

Although there have been great strides made in reducing gender inequality and violence against women, these are still ongoing issues. Every day, girls and women are faced with discrimination, abuse, and violence simply because they are female. But many believe it does not have to be this way. By taking violence against women seriously, people have the power to improve the way women around the world are treated.

Traditionally, advocates against violence have focused their efforts on responses and services for women who have been abused, according to UN Women. Given the harmful effects violence can have on women, this is understandable. But experts believe the best way to end violence against women is to prevent it from happening in the first place. "Prevention should start early in life, by educating and working with young boys and girls promoting respectful relationships and gender equality," according to UN Women. "Working with youth is a 'best bet' for faster, sustained progress on preventing and eradicating gender-based violence. While public policies and interventions often overlook this stage of life, it is a critical time when values and norms around gender equality are forged."[56] This means that people, communities, and governments must address the root causes of violence and the problems in society that make violence possible.

"Prevention [of violence] should start early in life, by educating and working with young boys and girls promoting respectful relationships and gender equality."[56]
– UN Women

SOURCE NOTES

INTRODUCTION: A SPOTLIGHT ON VIOLENCE AGAINST WOMEN

1. Jane Mayer and Ronan Farrow, "Four Women Accuse New York's Attorney General of Physical Abuse," *The New Yorker*, May 7, 2018. www.newyorker.com.

2. Quoted in Mayer and Farrow, "Four Women Accuse New York's Attorney General of Physical Abuse."

3. Quoted in Mayer and Farrow, "Four Women Accuse New York's Attorney General of Physical Abuse."

4. Quoted in Mayer and Farrow, "Four Women Accuse New York's Attorney General of Physical Abuse."

5. Quoted in Mayer and Farrow, "Four Women Accuse New York's Attorney General of Physical Abuse."

6. "Domestic Violence Myths and Truths," *SAFE*, n.d. www.safeaustin.org.

7. Quoted in Kyle Jones, "Rose McGowan Says Women Everywhere Face Abuse from Powerful Men in Their Lives," *Women in the World*, April 27, 2018. www.womenintheworld.com.

8. Quoted in Jones, "Rose McGowan Says Women Everywhere Face Abuse from Powerful Men in Their Lives."

9. Kate Manne, "Eric Schneiderman and the Meaning of Strangulation," *New York Times*, May 10, 2018. www.nytimes.com.

10. Quoted in Renee Morad, "Rose McGowan's Biggest #MeToo Worry," *NBC News*, February 9, 2018. www.nbcnews.com.

CHAPTER 1: WHAT IS THE HISTORY BEHIND VIOLENCE AGAINST WOMEN?

11. Quoted in Jonathan Yardley, "Book Review: 'Wedlock' by Wendy Moore," *Washington Post*, March 8, 2009. www.washingtonpost.com.

12. Quoted in Yardley, "Book Review: 'Wedlock' by Wendy Moore."

13. Quoted in Yardley, "Book Review: 'Wedlock' by Wendy Moore."

14. Quoted in Wendy Moore, "18th Century Domestic Violence," *Wonders and Marvels*, n.d. www.wondersandmarvels.com.

15. Quoted in Moore, "18th Century Domestic Violence."

16. Quoted in Moore, "18th Century Domestic Violence."

17. Ruth Rosen, "We Will Not Be Beaten," *50.50*, September 8, 2014. www.opendemocracy.net.

18. Quoted in Eliana Dockterman, "50 Years Ago, Doctors Called Domestic Violence 'Therapy,'" *Time,* September 25, 2014. www.time.com.

19. Quoted in Dockterman, "50 Years Ago, Doctors Called Domestic Violence 'Therapy.'"

20. Quoted in "What Is Violence Against Women?" *Jane Doe Inc.*, n.d. www.janedoe.org.

21. Quoted in "What Is Violence Against Women?"

22. "What Is Violence Against Women?"

23. "What Is Violence Against Women?"

24. Ashley Easter, "How Patriarchy in the Church Plays a Role in Abuse," *Relevant*, October 16, 2017. www.relevantmagazine.com.

25. Michael Kaufman, "The Seven P's of Men's Violence," *Articles on Ending Men's Violence*, 1999. www.michaelkaufman.com.

26. Kaufman, "The Seven P's of Men's Violence."

27. Kaufman, "The Seven P's of Men's Violence."

CHAPTER 2: WHAT TYPES OF VIOLENCE DO WOMEN FACE?

28. Emma Bogler, "Frustrated by Columbia's Inaction, Student Reports Sexual Assault to Police," *Columbia Daily Spectator*, December 28, 2016. www.columbiaspectator.com.

29. Quoted in Eun Kyung Kim, "Columbia Student Carrying Mattress to Protest Alleged Rape Gets 'Overwhelmingly Positive' Response," *Today*, October 14, 2016. www.today.com.

30. Quoted in Rande Iaboni, "Students Accuse Columbia University of Mishandling Sexual Assaults," *CNN*, May 1, 2014. www.cnn.com.

31. Quoted in Kim, "Columbia Student Carrying Mattress to Protest Alleged Rape Gets 'Overwhelmingly Positive' Response."

32. Quoted in Gabriella Paiella, "Emma Sulkowicz Received NOW's 2016 'Woman of Courage' Award," *The Cut*, June 28, 2016. www.thecut.com.

33. Manne, "Eric Schneiderman and the Meaning of Strangulation."

CHAPTER 3: WHAT ARE THE EFFECTS OF VIOLENCE AGAINST WOMEN?

34. Glenn McEntyre, "'Find Help, Run': Woman Set On Fire Shares Message For Abused Women," *10TV*, December 12, 2016. www.10tv.com.

35. McEntyre, "'Find Help, Run': Woman Set On Fire Shares Message For Abused Women."

36. Quoted in Glenn McEntyre, "Woman Set On Fire: Attacker's Punishment Doesn't Fit Crime," *10TV*, December 13, 2016. www.10tv.com.

37. Quoted in Chris Harris, "5 Things to Know About Judy Malinowski, Who Lived For Two Years After Being Set on Fire by Fiancé," *People*, June 28, 2017. www.people.com.

38. Quoted in McEntyre, "'Find Help, Run': Woman Set On Fire Shares Message For Abused Women."

39. Quoted in Ben Garbarek, "Slager Sentenced to Life in Prison for Ex-Girlfriend's Burning Death," *ABC 6 News*, July 5, 2018. www.abc6onyourside.com.

40. Quoted in Lauren Pelley, "Leaving Relationship Is 'Most Dangerous Time' For Domestic Violence Victims, Experts Say," *CBC News*, December 8, 2016. www.cbc.ca.

41. "Health Effects of Domestic Violence," *Stop Violence Against Women*, August 2013. www.stopvaw.org.

42. "Health Effects of Domestic Violence."

43. Quoted in "Health Effects of Domestic Violence."

44. Quoted in "Health Effects of Domestic Violence."

45. Quoted in "Health Effects of Domestic Violence."

46. Quoted in University of Montreal, "Impact of Domestic Violence on Women's Mental Health," *ScienceDaily*, March 31, 2015. www.sciencedaily.com.

47. Quoted in Michael Alison Chandler, "For Homeless Women, Violence Is a Pervasive Part of Their Past and Present, Report Shows," *Washington Post*, February 19, 2018. www.washingtonpost.com.

48. Quoted in Chandler, "For Homeless Women, Violence Is a Pervasive Part of Their Past and Present, Report Shows."

49. Lakshmi Puri, "The Economic Costs of Violence Against Women," *UN Women*, September 21, 2016. www.unwomen.org.

50. Puri, "The Economic Costs of Violence Against Women."

51. Puri, "The Economic Costs of Violence Against Women."

CHAPTER 4: HOW CAN VIOLENCE AGAINST WOMEN BE PREVENTED?

52. Quoted in Associated Press, "Justice Dept.: Violence Against Women Fell 64% Over Decade," *CBS News*, March 7, 2013. www.cbsnews.com.

53. Quoted in Associated Press, "Justice Dept.: Violence Against Women Fell 64% Over Decade."

54. Quoted in Associated Press, "Justice Dept.: Violence Against Women Fell 64% Over Decade."

55. "What Men Can Do to Help Stop Domestic Violence," *Domestic Violence Prevention Centre*, n.d. www.domesticviolence.com.au.

56. "Focusing on Prevention to Stop the Violence," *UN Women*, n.d. www.unwomen.org.

FOR FURTHER **RESEARCH**

BOOKS

Noah Berlatsky, *Sexual Violence*. Farmington Hills, MI: Greenhaven Press, 2014.

Ann Byers, *Sexual Assault and Abuse*. New York: Rosen Young Adult, 2015.

Sherri Mabry Gordon, *Are You Being Abused?* New York: Enslow
    Publishing, 2015.

Jack Lasky, *Sexual Assault on Campus*. Farmington Hills, MI: Greenhaven
    Press, 2016.

Noël Merino, *Violence Against Women*. Farmington Hills, MI: Greenhaven
    Press, 2016.

Carla Mooney, *Teen Violence*. San Diego, CA: ReferencePoint Press, 2013.

INTERNET SOURCES

Michael Alison Chandler, "For Homeless Women, Violence Is a Pervasive Part
    of Their Past and Present, Report Shows," *Washington Post*, February 19,
    2018. www.washingtonpost.com.

Christen A. Johnson and KT Hawbaker, "#MeToo: A Timeline of Events," *Chicago
    Tribune*, July 27, 2018. www.chicagotribune.com.

Kyle Jones, "Rose McGowan Says Women Everywhere Face Abuse from
    Powerful Men in Their Lives," *Women in the World*, April 27, 2018.
    www.womenintheworld.com.

WEBSITES

End Violence Against Women International
www.evawintl.org

This organization works to create a world where gender-based violence is unacceptable and where perpetrators are held accountable. It also strives to ensure victims receive the compassion, support, and justice they deserve.

Futures Without Violence
www.futureswithoutviolence.org

This nonprofit group provides programs, policies, and campaigns designed to empower individuals and organizations to end violence against women and children around the world.

National Center on Domestic and Sexual Violence
www.ncdsv.org

This organization provides and customizes trainings and consultations designed to end both domestic violence and sexual violence. It also influences national policies and promotes collaboration among groups with the sole purpose of ending violence.

UN Women
www.unwomen.org

This international group focuses on priority areas that are fundamental to women's equality, such as economic empowerment, ending violence, governance, and national planning. The goal is to promote progress in multiple areas across the board.

World Health Organization
www.who.int

More than 7,000 people from more than 150 countries work for this organization in an effort to promote the health and well-being of people around the world.

INDEX

IMAGE CREDITS

Cover: © kieferpix/iStockphoto

4: © Clive Chilvers/Shutterstock Images

5: © Shawn Goldberg/Shutterstock Images

8: © lev radin/Shutterstock Images

10: © Krista Kennell/Shutterstock Images

13: © Library of Congress

17: © RichLegg/iStockphoto

21: © Primeop76/iStockphoto

25: © Andrew Burton/Getty Images

30: © pecaphoto77/iStockphoto

32: © Lolostock/Shutterstock Images

35: © Antonio Guillem/Shutterstock Images

37: © Emilio Morenatti/AP Images

38: © Red Line Editorial

41: © John Gomez/Shutterstock Images

51: © RyanKing999/iStockphoto

54: © Pressmaster/Shutterstock Images

59: © Shawn Goldberg/Shutterstock Images

66: © AppleZoomZoom/Shutterstock Images

68: © Prostock-studio/Shutterstock Images

ABOUT THE AUTHOR

Sherri Mabry Gordon is a bullying prevention advocate and author of nearly twenty nonfiction books. Many of her books deal with issues teens face today, including bullying, abuse, public shaming, online safety, and more. Gordon also writes about bullying, relationships, and parenting for Verywell.com. She has given multiple presentations to schools, churches, and the YMCA on bullying prevention, dating abuse, and online safety, and she volunteers regularly. She also serves on the School Counselor Advisory Board for two schools. Gordon resides in Columbus, Ohio, with her husband, two children, and dog, Abbey.